spring clean

written by
sabreen islam

illustrated by
alice waldow

This is a work of fiction. Names, characters, places, and incidents either are the product of the author's imagination or are used fictitiously. Any resemblance to actual persons, living or dead, events, or locales is entirely coincidental.

Copyright © 2022 by Sabreen Islam

All rights reserved. No part of this book may be reproduced or used in any manner without written permission of the copyright owner except for the use of quotations in a book review.

Cover design copyright © 2022 by Alice Waldow
Illustrations copyright © 2022 by Alice Waldow

ISBN 978-0-473-60237-6 (paperback)
ISBN 978-0-473-60238-8 (ebook)

www.sabreenislam.squarespace.com

so here it has gathered
in the unseen corners
all the dust and photos and clutter
forgotten epiphanies
abandoned fairies in their jars
covered in cobwebs and lint
pain and scars
armed with a dust and pan
i say as i stand
'perhaps it is time
for a spring clean.'

— *spring clean*

Winter

we were so beautiful
like light and shade
sun-warmed and familiar
old photos of summer days

— *summer memories*

the glow faded
and the euphoria slowly died
shoulders curved inwards
shadows smudged under eyes
but still we hold on

you whisper
and i wonder
but still we hold on

as autumn blows its breath
and we begin to turn red and yellow
and lose
our
grip

—*fall*

you tell me stories
and i listen
you tell me your grief
and i listen
you tell me i am not enough
and i listen
you tell me to stay
and i listen

— *empathy hurts*

a storm brews at home
words slash holes in the walls
crying red tears
i tell you my sorrow
but all i get
is silence

— *tell me that you care*

it is not an easy thing to share
not a casual subject
to bring up in a conversation
unable to be whispered
behind a textbook
like so many other
school-girl secrets

'i think i am being abused.'

but it is even more brutal
soul-guttering
when you utter this bombshell
and are answered
with nothing

— *abuse*

'i am broken' she proclaims
tears running in an endless stream
i pat her back and tell her 'i am here'

but she misinterprets my words
and hands me all of her pieces

'fix them'
she orders
then storms off
leaving me to pick them up
forgetting my own

trying to fix her puzzle
until i can no longer tell the difference
between her broken pieces and mine

— 'more broken than you'

what
are
words
but
weapons
what
is
silence
but
a
sword

— *verbal abuse*

i wrote my mother a letter
left it in her hands as i boarded the bus
all of the words
i did not have the courage to say
i wonder if
she had the courage to read them

— *does she know what she is doing?*

my hands
heart
soul
body
mind
all shake when i ask for something

— *anxiety*

because you are not in my photographs
and you demand why
but i have not admitted yet that i do not want you
there
so i lie

— *exclusion*

i sometimes wonder
how your voice does not tire
from the unending poison
flowing forth like a river

as tides pass with time
i marvel at your words
while a small voice
ponders in my mind
what happened to mine?

— *but i shut her up*

who says you can't deal with the hurt
by pouring it into pretty bottles
and locking them away?

— *bottling up*

my best friend is a living flame
she burns and flickers and waxes and wanes
she asks me where i have gone
what happened to my songs
to make them so sad?
from somewhere within i hear a distant cry
but i smile and tell her that i'm alright

— *lying is easier*

i do not understand rage.
how can one be so full of fury
when the grass grows
and the moon glows
why are you complaining
when you've got the whole world and more?

— *the wound is within*

i hide my words
when i see them coming
tuck away my melodies
put down my guitar
wipe away all signs of living
preparing for the next scar

— *survival*

                                                                        i do not know
where i have gone
all i know is
i am no longer afraid of the dark
it is quiet and watchful
peaceful and primitive
i am only afraid of
what lurks within it

— *the dark is innocent*

you are an anchor
disguised as a rope

this is not who we used to be.

the quiet is not limited to you
we have all lost our smiles
they are few and far between
we have become mountains
cold and rooted
unable to leave

— *hurt becomes normalised*

trust is a luxury
safety is a scam
keep your wits about you
and run while you can

— *running*

                                        she
                                     strikes
                                         in
                                        the
                                      night
                                          i
                                      never
                                        see
                                        her
                                    coming

                           — *shadows of my home*

to say it was all bad would be a lie
many wonderful things happened
in those months
little flowers of hope and happiness
that kept me sustained
but i hid them from you
because you were none of them

— *many wonderful things*

you need a punching bag
i am just what is nearest
and least likely to say anything

— *taking advantage of submission*

my parents taught me to say sorry
if i hurt someone
so when i hurt you, i said sorry
when you hurt me you made excuses
twisting it to make it matter less
so i said sorry
sorry
sorry
until i took all of yours
and said them for you

— *i am sorry to myself*

you and i
both blame me

i am too tired to be angry.

my family demands at the dinner table
asking why i am so quiet
i smile and say i have a headache

'take a Panadol after dinner' ma tells me
and the conversation shifts away
as i wordlessly swirl my rice with my fingers
wondering where all the noise inside me has gone

— *the universe has quieted*

it's been so long
since you last asked me
'how are you?'
and even longer
since i asked myself

— *niceties*

winter is here to stay. you don't see our friends
breaking. i do. i see their wilted shoulders and
starless eyes. the way they droop under the weight
of their burdens. you cannot see how much they
sacrifice for you.

i am not strong enough to be angry for me
but i love them enough to be angry for them

— *blind*

to this day i do not know
if you actually wanted me there
or if you just didn't want to be
alone

— *mutual solitude*

i
have
forgotten
what
being
okay
feels
like
there is only
seething silence
whispered violence
and bitter regret

you are always there
yet not
where are you
where are you not?

you've disappeared somewhere
i can't find you
where have you gone?

we cracked

and cracked

until we

inevitably

fell apart

.

.

.

you
are
gone
but
i
am
still
here

— *vanishing act*

i do not know what to do with myself
sitting here without you
with the watery sunlight
shining through the trees
brushing gentle fingers
across my wet cheeks
part of me wants to run
afraid i do not deserve it
but i stay
and feel it
gently caress over my face

— *sunrise*

i don't know
if i want
to be here
anymore
but the sky
wants me
to be here
so i think
i shall stay

— *force of nature*

in the weeks without you
i started drinking tea
watched the milk bloom
in the deep red
every morning
i kept a diary
i went outside
and bit by bit
i started to feel alive

— *tea*

is it bad if now
the world seems
a little brighter
a little more
awake?
should i feel guilty
to bask in the sun
that rose
after you left?
should i feel guilty
to feel good
now that you're gone?

— *turn the page*

things changed
became sweeter
without you there
to consume it
in darkness
and despair
the birds sing
the toaster pings
and i am here to witness them

— *mornings*

i
want
to
know
what
a
soft
sunrise
tastes
like

— *waking up earlier*

has the world always been this way?
so gently captivating
so softly warm?
did the grass always glow this way?
did the clouds always drift this way?
i spent so long
embroiled in you
i did not see
all of these wonders at my feet

— *it's the little things*

one

forward　　　　　　　　　　step

steps　　　　　　　　　　　two

to　　　　　　　　　　　　back

　　　　　　　　　　　　　you

— *but you are behind me now*

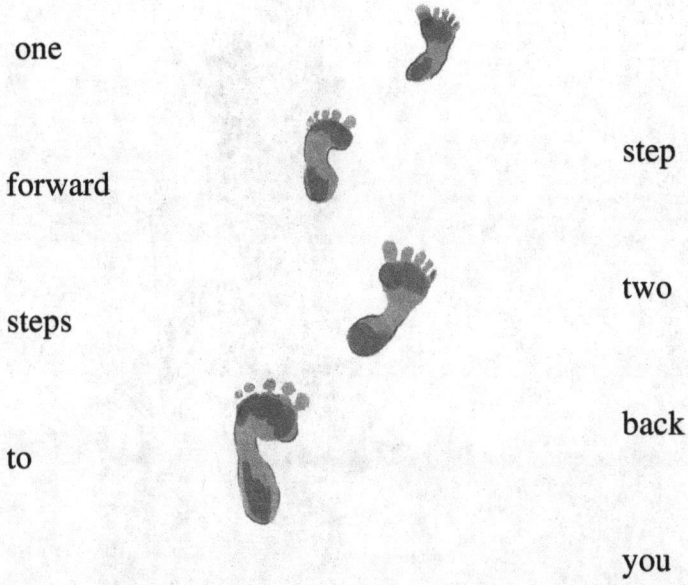

we communicate
in gilded words
neither of us
want to say aloud

— *poetry*

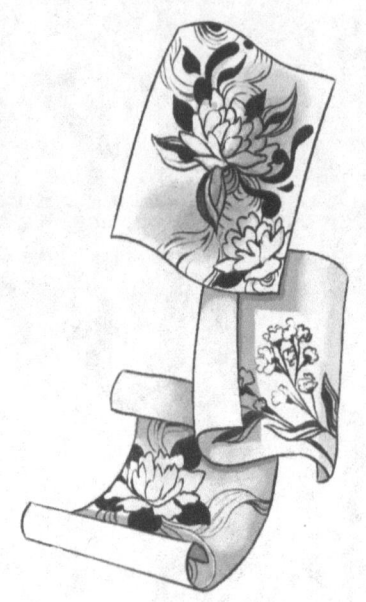

sometimes i wonder
do you miss me?
do you think of the happy times
before those months of agony?

do you ever want to laugh with me again?
could we ever do that?
we knew each other
can we un-know those intricacies?

i know now that
i can unwire you from my brain
but i don't know if i want to

— *we were friends once upon a time*

you put shackles around my feet
 but you were scared
because i had the key

— *i am stronger than you think*

my thoughts are moving away from you
carving new pathways
to sunnier, happier destinations
flowery fields
gentle woods
my favourite beach
i'm packing my bags
a holiday for one
digging my hands
into sun-warmed sands
so many things
i had planned
now i only have one:
to do all of them

— *bucket list*

i got on a boat to see my friend
walked under red brick buildings
and over silver metal bridges
i sat surrounded by other wayfarers
all headed somewhere
across the vibrant afternoon sea
i watch it flicker and splash
and playfully wave
as the yellow sun lovingly gazed
aboard this white floating contraption
in the middle of the sea
is this what it feels like
to be free?

—*ferry*

perhaps the clue
they are so scared for you to find
is that someday, somehow
you will be alright

but they will hold on and fight
clip your wings from flight
because they know that day is when
you are without them

— *the one that got away*

now that all the dust is gathered
i begin to clean

i will sweep up all
that no longer belongs to me
and throw it out into the sea
i will mop up your memory
and the tears it pried from my eyes
use them to fertilise
the sunflowers i have planted inside

this will no longer be
a tangle of weeds and woe
only good things will grow here
happiness and hope

i will light up my dark corners
with golden fairy lights
so that they may be a sanctuary
not a prison
when i need to cry

this will no longer be a place
i need to hide
this shall be henceforth be
my space to thrive

— *mind, body and soul*

i
have
been
closed
shut
for
so
long

i
wonder
what
would
happen
now
if
i
bloom

— *winter is ending*

Spring

my best friend
took me on a getaway

we drove through the green hills
that rolled into the wide blue sea

it was cold and i loved it
my black dress fluttered
about my knees
we danced and we sang
laughed and laughed again

my lips ached but i couldn't stop
my grin rose above
i wonder if that was freedom i felt
fitting just like a glove

— *we are born to be free*

find those
who will find you
when you thought
 you had lost yourself

— *helping hearts*

how the world sighs
when the clouds move
and the sun shines again

— *but it shone behind them anyway*

perhaps
who we grew to be
no longer fits
who we used to be
the years wrought
their cruel changes
on us differently

our love was drowning
in wishful thinking
you only lifted me up
when you needed me
shone a mirror on the ocean
so i thought i was flying

so it is with a heavy heart
i bid you goodbye
for you are no longer
the love of my life

— *one-way lover*

i did not know
one could wake up
calm and cloudy
to the smell of coffee
and rain on concrete
thursday humming
a song sweet and sleepy

i did not know
one did not have to
burst into the morning
bright and blinding
to the smell of gold
and promised wealth
emboldened in
capital letters
an extravaganza
at six am
the inevitable rise
to the impossible fall

or that one did not have to wake
to lightning on their tongue
smelling storms in the air
bracing for a hurricane
putting up barricades
before leaving home
black clouds chanting cheers
that sound just like
your whispered fears

i think i should like to be
calm and cloudy
not a golden glitter
kaleidoscope
not a looming lurking
thunderstorm
not a spring doomed
to ping pong between
euphoria and depression

i think
i should like to wake
to the smell of coffee
and the sounds of thursday
than to typhoons
or firework displays

calm and cloudy
you are the kind
of morning
that is just right
for me

— *calm and cloudy*

i thought it was selfish
to direct my own love within
little did i know
it is the only way to live

— *self-love*

sometimes
holding on hurts
more than
letting go

i kiss my stiff fingers
that were burned
by your rope

— *i held onto you*

clearing
you
away
feels
so
much
better
than
having
you
stay

— *unexpected ease*

i still hesitate
to feel safe
in the arms of those i love

because i am not used to this
this equal bond
still expecting you to take
still waiting to run away
like a wave poised to break

but the water ripples
hugs the sand and fades
as the final barrier melts
and you hold me anyway

— *opening up*

those who love you
will not make you beg
for them to stay.

i hate this. being afraid of you. i am sick and afraid and sick of being afraid of y – o – u. only now am i starting to realise what you did to me for months and months and i am *livid*. i want to scream at you. i want to shake you and force you to realise just how much of me you shattered. how you got under my skin and stayed there, infecting every thought and step i took. i want to spit venom at you – i want you to feel ashamed for what you did to me. but i will not.

i am not you
i will not let myself become you
i will not twist myself into something i am not
to relieve some temporary satisfaction

i will take the longer road
the harder road
to forgiveness and letting go

here i stand at the fork
of the two coasts
you were good to me once
i do believe that

but i will not give you
that final bit of power.

— *full stop on my anger*

i want to make my heart so full
that there is simply no room for you

i began to lean on those
who have always
been close
loudly
silently
the roots of my tree

how we have grown
my little flowers
i will hold you
as you have held me

nestle into me
because i love you
and i will nestle into you
because you love me

— *the nest*

alice is wide shoulders
the smell of chlorine
up at five am swimming
seeing the beauty in everything

she is soft golden hair
and kind green eyes
calloused hands
capture the night sky

ever humble about the medals
she wins for her victories
bright plans for the future
that she wears like jewellery

a lion with a heart of gold

— *the painter*

caitlyn is the softest
moonlight
the cashmere coat
to brave the night
a constant within
constant chaos
her soul is what stars
are made of

come
sit with me
watch her glow
the hearth that crackles
with the gentlest hope

for even when
the world goes cold
she will be there
guiding you home

— *the poet*

summer is kind eyes and smiles
on her all of the little stars shine

delicate hands
and indigo sands
clouds of golden hair
she is a soft
winter morning

a rainbow glimmers within her
unapologetic and bright
a promise that stays
during the dark night

she is the twinkling piano
hidden in a song
that diligently plays all along

a brave heart beating quiet and strong

— *the artist*

arabella is iced coffee
at six in the morning
startling and sweet
you might end up falling

she is a galaxy
in a little blue car
trouble focusing
in history class
always the first
and always the last

friends with everyone
knows your favourite song
her smile alone
sparks a firework show

life of the party
she lights up the room
rare and exciting
like spring's first bloom

— *the muse*

i am so grateful that
you exist
thank you
for being so
exactly
brilliantly
wonderfully
you

— *i love you*

i will hang your smiles on my wall
polaroids new and old
you shall decorate my headspace
a glittering gallery of memories

— *redecorating*

how strange it is
the word 'you'
it can be said
with all the smiles
or all the sadness
in the world
how is it
that 'you' could be
seven billion different people
all meaning
seven billion different things

  — *we live in a big world*

my songs are returning to me
sunny little melodies
flocking home like sweet birds
come back home my lovelies
aren't you a sight for sore eyes?
return to me
intertwine with my days
i'm grateful for however long you stay

the flowers are growing

the weather is changing

and with the seasons

i can feel your ice melting

— *i am growing out of you*

how interesting to see you again
my old friend
yet another ending
cloaking a beginning?

— *there are only beginnings*

i forgot what this felt like
quiet happiness
sitting down with time to think

because life was good today

maybe yesterday was hard
maybe this day wasn't extraordinary
but for the first time in a while
i look forward to the next

holding hands with that
promise of tomorrow
let it take me with it
like a child trailing a floating
balloon…

                                    i crash and burn
                                  but i will learn
               my falls will be spectacular
                                      waterfalls
                                            starfall
                    constellations tumbling
                        from their strings
                  the heavens raining down
                  in an effervescent cascade
                 and if this is only my fall
              wait until you see my rise

                    — *the truth about tribulations*

i have made so many memories
all adorned with golden fairy lights
and strings and frames and boxes of polaroids
twining through their midst
lilac walls
and wooden floors
witness it all

look around you
open your eyes
i promise you will see so many reasons
why you are so lucky to be alive

— *awakening*

there is a wild ocean
beneath this fair façade
of which she is
the sole wanderer
bound to explore
its icy depths forever

you will never see
the darkness inside
of her
but you will
never witness
the sunken treasures
either

— *tip of the iceberg*

every item in my wardrobe
is some shade of blue

indigo
cobalt
blueberry
sea-salt

all shades of blue
and whatever i buy
i still choose
blue

there's something
about it
something
magnanimous
and i've tried
other colours
but none seem
to fit

like a slip of sky
from far above
a drop of ocean
to the call of gulls
a swirling tempest
in the mists of may
a quiet rain
on a hazy day

everything in my wardrobe
is monochrome
and i like it
that way
i like me
in blue

— *monochrome*

                                                    i
                                               never
                                               knew
                                                i'd
                                              taste
                                          freedom
                                          without
                                                you

but
it rolled out
in front of me
like a golden carpet
after you left

                         even the world stopped hurting
                              the birds started singing
                           the swords fell out of the walls
                    the wounds at home gently healed over
                                    it was like you leaving
                              was a band-aid ripped clean

so
in a strange way
thank you for leaving
for doing it when i
couldn't

thank you for leaving my world
so it could be sweet again
thank you for leaving
because it led me here

i look back at the girl
who survived
the wolves disguised as fairy godmothers
the dark woods with a phantom sun
the pain lacing every song

i look back at the girl
who had to shed her innocence
far too soon
whose trust was broken
over and over
glass hope shattered in the cold
who mastered invisibility
and wore it as a tattered cloak

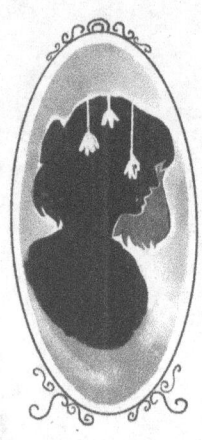

walking with soundless steps
through forest fires as they raged
lost where she was getting to
just trying to get through

i look back to the girl i was
who lived as a ghost for months
hope was a dream
she didn't dare believe
only trusting her feet

i look back at her
just barely holding on
and suddenly realise
behind those frightened eyes
there was a wolf inside
destined to survive

i look back at her
wandering lost through those woods
and though she cannot hear me
i whisper to her

'soon, my darling
there is a place you are getting to
that you don't know yet
trust your feet
and you will feel the sun again'

she looks at me with tired eyes
the portrait of the hopelessly resigned
nodding her head to save her time

dear girl
i promise that i will remember you
i will not brush over you
because you were me
and i was you

i promise that i will honour you
because you were the one
who lived through that time
though you lost hope
it was still there
ever so quietly
leading you here

— *to those months of despair*

this is how i know
there is most definitely a god
a kind presence watching over us
righting the wrongs

how else could all of this
magnificence exist?
it's old and gentle
magic in our midst

the stories and myths
i believe all of them
o Allah be with me
every day that i live

— *religion*

books are mystical creatures
unwitting hearts beware
you only need a glimpse
to be snared
by worlds created by those
who walk among you

page by page
they will devour you
take you to places
your heart will ache for
to lifetimes and galaxies
great wars and adventurers

join them on their journeys
watch as they grow
it is the same magic
we felt as five-year-olds
listening to fairy tales

— *all my heart desires*

so here we sit
on a windy november night
perched on the top of the stairs
waiting for fireworks
to light up the dark
we hold our breath
and gasp when they display
but i love these
precious minutes more
as we wait
on the stairs
in the dark
just us two
waiting for the sky to bloom

— *Guy Fawkes's Day*

maybe we are all just fireworks
waiting for our turn to burst
and when we do
we light up the sky
shooting high
burning bright
for one glorious existence
over in the blink of an eye
cascading back down to earth
every moment from our birth
we bloom like flowers
all of one second
in this universe
is ours

so make it count.

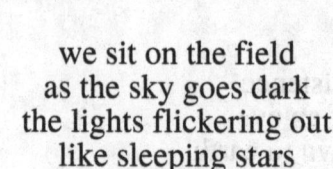

we sit on the field
as the sky goes dark
the lights flickering out
like sleeping stars

all things
seem to be fading
blooming backwards
the classrooms close
their windows
the flowers close
their petals

'i don't want things to change'
you say
'i want to stay'

i hold your hand
it's grass stained
with splattered paint
from memories we've made
in this place

my heart strains
as time turns our page
past the happy ending
just as we've found our footing

'i know'
i say after a while
'but look how pretty the sky is'

— *dusk*

i now see that we were both lost
you lost your way too
i only ever wanted to find you

i will take our good memories
and keep them where they are
but no further

                              i wish you every happiness

                              i hope all your dreams come true

                              and i pray that one day

                              you will look up

                              let forgiveness find you

                              as it found me

                              let the rainstorms make you clean

                              and count all of your blessings

before they disappear.

— *forgiveness*

hope
it is a golden-winged thing
who sat on my shoulder
for so many years

she guided me
through despair and dismay
but at one point i lost her
and i will never forget
that emptiness
those gaping months
of nothing and nothing
though i no longer fear
their memory

so though she was with me
for most of my life
now i thank the heavens and skies
because i lived the world with her
and glimpsed the world without her
and realised i had been blind

now her gentle touch gilds everything
i didn't see before
golden light glimmering
under every closed door

if we let her illuminate existence
then maybe we could see
how only she is stronger than fear
this little winged thing

— *hope has wings* :)

fly little butterfly
fly wide and strong
for your wings are free
and the road is long

— *flight*

perhaps hardship does not make you dirty
but clean
perhaps struggle does not make you weak
but strong
perhaps being soft does not make you foolish
but powerful

and perhaps dreaming between the madness
of a better world
a good world
between the sorrow and tears and joy
does not make you unworthy of it
but is a prelude to it
destiny's pre-chorus
a fated cadence.

and if you lose hope…

perhaps that does not mean
you are defeated
but willing to wait
for however long it may be
however long you need to take

before you take a deep breath
pick up a rubbish bag
and begin to throw all
the long-rusted things in
a spring clean, of sorts
to take what no longer
belongs in your heart
and let it go.

clear out the room and all that is cluttered there
open up the window and let in the fresh air
let it refresh your soul and its now freed up space
promise you of the better things that will take their
place

feel the wind against your dreams
listen to them sing
their voices clear now that the noise is gone
how wonderful they sound
when given the microphone

see all the good memories
your purest foundations
lighting the space
a night sky of precious moments
their constellations no longer
swallowed up by the dark

sit beneath them and remind yourself
of all you have done
and imagine how your best
is probably yet to come
let that sink in
that unwavering promise…

then get up
tie up the bag of flotsam
and wreckage
walk down the stairs
out the door
and chuck it out

turn around
do not look back
only to that shining night sky
waiting for you

then walk up into it
let yourself be surrounded
by the peace of the open universe
within yourself now

take your time
reacquaint yourself like old friends
to who you are
who you've been
and who you will be
the three most important people
you'll ever meet

lazily swim about this unending galaxy
clean of the space pollution that crowded it
dive into its depths
explore its every beautiful reach
wink at the nebulas and be glad for them
for a star has died
and been reborn

this is your space
know that now
and forever
this is your universe
to think it only needed a little dusting
but it never stops giving
never stops living
even after you do

so memorise it
dance through it
run your hands and fingers through it
marvel at it
marvel at you
for this is your self
in all its blazing, quiet
hidden beauty

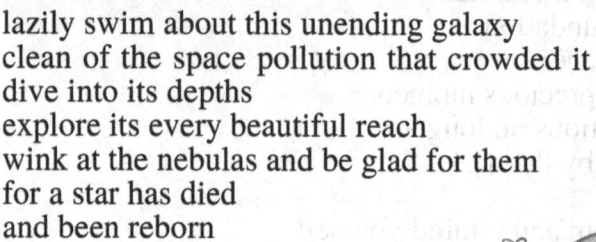

this starry, starry night
this effervescent might
this is your universe
a you-niverse.

— *it really just needed some dusting*

now i am done
cleaning through everything
unnecessary baggage and junk
thrown out
discarded

anything that could be hurtful
in my beautiful world
is gone
only those that deserve
to take up precious space
remain

the dust is gone
like the snow of winter
dew in the sun

now i shall grow
as summer sighs near
the sun shines clear
my spring clean ends

though i have no doubt
i will clean again
but now i know i can do it
and that's halfway there

so strange to find a universe within
when there was only darkness for some time

i suppose that's all there can be
until someone turns on the light.

— *spring clean II*

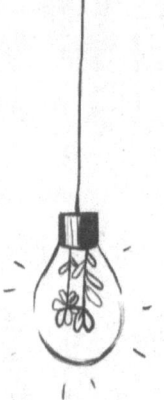

The End

acknowledgments

when i first wrote *spring clean*, i was fifteen years old, reeling from toxic relationships and experiences of abuse. this was my lifeline in the months that followed, as i tried to process what had happened to me, carefully piecing my reality back together until it resembled something close to how i was feeling. now, nearing twenty, my heart overflows with pride and joy for this project and what it means to me.

it could not have happened without the special people in my life who have shaped who i am. to ma and baba, thank you for letting me dream wildly and limitlessly. thank you for listening to me, for raising me, for making me endless cups of *cha* and coming to every show i play without complaint; for posting even my most mundane achievement on facebook with the same amount of pride as my highest one. to my sisters, thank you for putting up with me. thank you for teasing me relentlessly about a lisp i adamantly refuse to have, and making me laugh when i thought i'd never smile again. to my cats — all three of you, with another addition since i first wrote this book — thank you for existing. i don't think you can read, but you're in here anyway.

to my precious high school teachers. as cheesy as it seems, you really did save my life. thank you for letting me stumble in twenty minutes late, for letting me ugly-sob to you after class, for letting me stay in your classrooms as a safe space when i had nowhere else to go. i wish i could repay you.

to ms zinn, thank you for believing in this book more than anyone i know. to mr baker, thank you for looking after me and rambling about history with me.

to mr worsnop, thank you for your endless dad jokes and creating a safe space during a time in my life when safety was rare. i owe you all so much.

to margaret, lorraine and everyone at lighthouse PR: thank you for taking a chance on me!

to my friends. we've come a long way since i first wrote these words. i love you and miss you all so much. summer, thank you for all those lunchtimes and hours we spent hiding away in band practice rooms. larry, thank you for making me laugh, looking after me and being the extrovert who adopted me. caitlyn, thank you for carrying me through those disastrous years and now, for every lord of the rings marathon, for every freak out about taylor swift. i love you more than you will ever know.

and finally, alice. we fucking did it buddy. this is our baby. if the words existed to convey the gratitude and awe i have for you i would write them a thousand times over. thank you for lending your incredible talent and beautiful mind to this little blue book. thank you for making my life better for the eight years i've known you. you have been here through timezone differences, my nightmares and dreams coming true, some truly horrendous haircuts and people, and everything else. i do not know where or who i would be without you. you deserve the world.

to readers: thank you for picking up this book. i wish i could hug every single one of you and will make it my life mission to do so. i wish you so much peace and joy, and i hope all of your dreams come true. see you soon!

about the author

Sabreen Islam has been writing ever since she learned how to. Born in Auckland, New Zealand, to Bengali parents, she grew up watching the world around her and writing it all down, through songs, stories and poetry. When she is not writing, Sabreen can be found with her guitar or other instrument, or scrambling to finish work to get back to her music or writing.

Sabreen lives in Auckland with her family and three cats, who have encouraged her to dream since day one. She is an aspiring author and singer-songwriter, and is currently studying a Bachelor of Laws and Arts at the University of Auckland. This is Sabreen's first published book.

about the author

Subicap Island has been writing over since she could read, now from her home on the Island, New Zealand to Bengali parents. She grew up watching the world around her and writing it all down, through songs, stories and books. When she is not writing, Sabreen can be found with her guitar or other instrument, scrambling to finish a work or get back to her multiple writings.

Sabreen lives in Auckland with her family, and three cats, who have encouraged her to live in peace daily. She is an aspiring author and singer-songwriter and is currently studying a bachelor of Laws and Arts at the University of Auckland. The Book of Sabh is her first published book.

*and for the dreamers
the reckless, wild believers
for those who feel just
a little more than the rest
who fall
and fall
again and again
to the painters, the poets
the artists and muses
for those who are magic
who make this world
a little brighter
this is for you.*

— dedication

www.ingramcontent.com/pod-product-compliance
Lightning Source LLC
Chambersburg PA
CBHW011151290426
44109CB00025B/2567